Table Of Contents

Chapter 2: Setting Up Your Environment 1
Chapter 3: Building the Game Framework 1
Chapter 4: Programming Sprites 1
Chapter 5: Programming the Background 1
Chapter 6: Adding Gameplay Elements 1
Chapter 7: Enhancing Visuals and Audio 1
Chapter 8: Saving and Loading Progress 1
Chapter 9: Expanding the Game 1
Chapter 10: Polishing and Releasing Your RPG 1
Chapter 11: Learning and Growing as a Game Developer 1
Chapter 12: Exploring New Horizons in Game Development 1
Chapter 1: Introduction 1

Create your own mind-blowing ultimate RPG

By: Chip Ziem

1. Introduction

- Overview of RPGs and their components.

- Why Python and PyCharm are great for game development.
- Prerequisites (Python basics, PyCharm installation, Pygame library).

2. Setting Up Your Environment

- Installing Python and PyCharm.
- Setting up a virtual environment.
- Installing the Pygame library.
- Creating the project structure (folders for assets, scripts, etc.).

3. Building the Game Framework

- Setting up the main game loop.
- Handling events (keyboard and mouse input).
- Updating the game state and rendering.

4. Programming Sprites

- Creating sprite classes for:
    - Heroes: Player-controlled characters.
    - Villains: AI-controlled enemies.
    - Extra Characters: NPCs with interactions.
- Adding movement, animations, and interactions.

5. Creating the Background

- Designing and loading backgrounds (static and scrolling).
- Layering backgrounds for depth (parallax scrolling).
- Using tilesets for modular background design.

6. Adding Gameplay Elements

- Collision detection for characters and obstacles.
- Health bars, score systems, and inventory.

- Dialog systems for story progression.

7. Enhancing Visuals and Audio

- Adding visual effects (e.g., explosions, spells).
- Incorporating sound effects and background music.
- Using Pygame's mixer for audio handling.

8. Saving and Loading Progress

- Storing game state (saving hero stats, inventory, and progress).
- Loading saved data.

9. Testing and Debugging

- Debugging tips in PyCharm.
- Common issues and how to resolve them.

10. Expanding the Game

- Ideas for levels, quests, and additional features.
- Modularizing code for scalability.

11. Complete Sample Code

A fully functional mini-RPG example with heroes, villains, extra characters, and backgrounds.

12. Conclusion

- Encouragement for further exploration.
- Resources for learning advanced game development.

Chapter 1: Introduction

1.1 What is an RPG?

A Role-Playing Game (RPG) is a genre of game where players assume the roles of characters in a fictional setting. Players often control their characters' actions and decisions to advance through a storyline, overcome challenges, and achieve goals. Key elements of RPGs include:

- Characters: Heroes, villains, and supporting characters, each with unique attributes.
- Story: A plot that guides the player's journey through the game.
- World: A rich environment where the adventure takes place.
- Interaction: The player's ability to engage with the world and its inhabitants.

Popular RPGs include games like Final Fantasy, The Witcher, and Pokemon. In this e-book, we will create a simple 2D RPG that demonstrates these core elements.

1.2 Why Use Python for RPG Development?

Python is an excellent language for game development due to its simplicity and readability, making it beginner-friendly. Additionally, Python has powerful libraries like Pygame, which is specifically designed for 2D game development. Here's why Python is a great choice:

- Easy to learn: Python's syntax is straightforward and intuitive, making it accessible even for beginners.
- Active community: Python has a vast community, so finding help and resources is easy.
- Pygame library: Pygame simplifies many game development tasks, such as rendering graphics, handling user input, and playing audio.

1.3 Why Use PyCharm?

PyCharm is a professional Integrated Development Environment (IDE) for Python that offers many features to streamline game development:

- Code completion: Saves time by suggesting code as you type.
- Debugging tools: Helps identify and fix errors quickly.
- Project organization: Keeps your files and assets structured and manageable.
- Virtual environment support: Simplifies the process of installing and managing dependencies like Pygame.

1.4 What Will You Learn in This E-Book?

This e-book will guide you through the process of creating a 2D RPG from scratch using Python and PyCharm. You'll learn how to:

- Set up your development environment.
- Create characters (heroes, villains, and extras) with animations and attributes.
- Build interactive backgrounds for your game world.
- Implement gameplay mechanics like movement, collisions, and dialog.
- Add visual and audio elements to enhance your game.

By the end, you'll have a working RPG prototype and the knowledge to expand it further.

1.5 What Do You Need to Get Started?

Before diving in, ensure you have the following:

1. Python Installed: Download and install Python from python.org.
2. PyCharm Installed: Download PyCharm (Community Edition is free) from jetbrains.com/pycharm.

3. Pygame Library: Install Pygame using the command:

   bash

   Copy code

   pip install pygame

4. Basic Python Knowledge: Familiarity with Python basics like variables, loops, and functions will be helpful.

1.6 Project Goals

The game we'll build will include:

- A hero sprite that the player controls.
- Villain sprites with basic AI behavior.
- A rich background with interactive elements.
- Core gameplay mechanics like movement, combat, and dialog.

Chapter 2: Setting Up Your Environment

Before we start coding, we need to prepare our development environment. This chapter will guide you through installing the necessary tools and organizing your project.

2.1 Installing Python

Python is the programming language we'll use for this RPG. Follow these steps to install it:

1. Visit the Python website.
2. Download the latest version of Python for your operating system.

3. Run the installer. Make sure to check the box that says "Add Python to PATH" before clicking "Install."

4. After installation, verify Python is installed by opening a terminal or command prompt and typing:

```bash
```

Copy code

```
python --version
```

This should display the installed Python version.

2.2 Installing PyCharm

PyCharm is the IDE we'll use for development. Follow these steps to set it up:

1. Visit the PyCharm website.
2. Download the Community Edition (free version).
3. Install PyCharm by following the instructions for your operating system.
4. Launch PyCharm and configure the default settings.

2.3 Installing the Pygame Library

Pygame is a Python library designed for game development. To install it:

1. Open a terminal or command prompt.

2. Run the following command:

```bash
```

Copy code

pip install pygame

3. Verify the installation by typing:

```bash
```

Copy code

python -m pygame --version

This should display the installed version of Pygame.

2.4 Setting Up Your PyCharm Project

Now, let's set up a project for our RPG:

1. Open PyCharm.
2. Click on "New Project" and select a location for your project.
3. In the "Interpreter" section, click "Add New Interpreter", then choose "Virtual Environment". This ensures that all dependencies for this project are isolated.
4. Click "Create" to set up the project.

2.5 Organizing Your Project

A well-organized project structure makes development easier. Create the following folders in your PyCharm project:

```css
```

Copy code

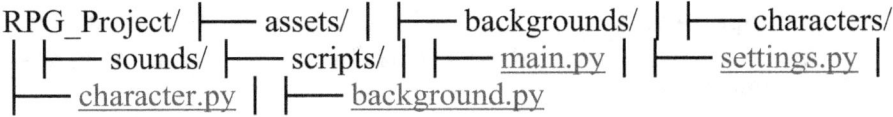

- assets/: Stores all game assets (images, sounds, etc.).

    o backgrounds/: Contains background images for the game.
    o characters/: Contains sprite images for heroes, villains, and extras.
    o sounds/: Contains sound effects and music.

- scripts/: Contains Python scripts for different parts of the game.

    o main.py: The entry point of the game.
    o settings.py: Stores global game settings (e.g., screen size, frame rate).
    o character.py: Contains classes and functions for characters.
    o background.py: Handles background rendering and interaction.

2.6 Setting Up Your First Script

Let's create the main game loop in main.py to ensure everything is working:

1. Open main.py in the scripts/ folder.

2. Add the following code:

    python

    Copy code

```
import pygame import sys # Initialize Pygame pygame.init()
# Screen settings SCREEN_WIDTH, SCREEN_HEIGHT =
800, 600 screen =
pygame.display.set_mode((SCREEN_WIDTH,
SCREEN_HEIGHT)) pygame.display.set_caption("RPG
Game") # Main game loop def main(): clock =
pygame.time.Clock() running = True while running: for
event in pygame.event.get(): if event.type == pygame.QUIT:
running = False # Fill the screen with a color screen.fill((0, 0,
0)) # Update the display pygame.display.flip() # Limit the
frame rate clock.tick(60) pygame.quit() sys.exit() if name ==
"__main__": main()
```

3. Run the script by clicking the green play button in PyCharm.

You should see a black window appear. This is the game window, and it confirms that your setup is working correctly.

2.7 Testing the Setup

Before moving forward, ensure the following:

- The game window opens without errors.
- You see a black screen with a title "RPG Game."
- The window closes correctly when you click the "X" button.

If you encounter any errors, double-check your Python, Pygame, and PyCharm installation.

Chapter 3: Building the Game Framework

In this chapter, we'll create the basic structure of our RPG. This includes setting up the game loop, handling events like user input, and preparing the foundation for game elements such as sprites and backgrounds.

3.1 Understanding the Game Loop

The game loop is the core of any game. It continuously runs to process events, update the game state, and render the game visuals. Here's how it works:

1. Event Handling: Processes user input, such as keyboard or mouse actions.
2. Game Logic Updates: Updates the state of the game, such as character positions or animations.
3. Rendering: Draws the game visuals to the screen.

3.2 Setting Up the Framework

Let's extend the main.py script to include the foundational game framework:

1. Open main.py.

2. Update it with the following code:

    python

    Copy code

    import pygame import sys # Initialize Pygame pygame.init() # Screen settings SCREEN_WIDTH, SCREEN_HEIGHT = 800, 600 screen = pygame.display.set_mode((SCREEN_WIDTH, SCREEN_HEIGHT)) pygame.display.set_caption("RPG Game") # Colors BLACK = (0, 0, 0) WHITE = (255, 255, 255) # Frame rate FPS = 60 # Main game loop def main(): clock = pygame.time.Clock() running = True while running: # Event handling for event in pygame.event.get(): if event.type == pygame.QUIT: running = False # Game logic (to be added later) # Rendering screen.fill(BLACK) # Clear the screen with a black background pygame.display.flip() # Update the display # Limit the frame rate clock.tick(FPS) pygame.quit() sys.exit() if name == "__main__": main()

3. Run the script. You should see a black screen that responds to the close button.

3.3 Handling User Input

Player interaction is crucial for an RPG. Let's modify the game loop to handle basic keyboard input:

1. Add a section to handle keyboard input:

    python

    Copy code

    # Event handling for event in pygame.event.get(): if event.type == pygame.QUIT: running = False elif event.type == pygame.KEYDOWN: if event.key == pygame.K_UP: print("Up arrow pressed") elif event.key == pygame.K_DOWN: print("Down arrow pressed") elif event.key == pygame.K_LEFT: print("Left arrow pressed") elif event.key == pygame.K_RIGHT: print("Right arrow pressed")

2. Run the game and press the arrow keys. The corresponding direction should print in the console.

3.4 Creating a Settings File

To make our game easier to manage, let's create a settings.py file to store global configurations:

1. Create a new file in the scripts/ folder called settings.py.

2. Add the following code:

    python

Copy code

```
# Screen settings
SCREEN_WIDTH = 800
SCREEN_HEIGHT = 600
FPS = 60
# Colors
BLACK = (0, 0, 0)
WHITE = (255, 255, 255)
```

3. Update main.py to use the settings:

python

Copy code

```
from settings import SCREEN_WIDTH, SCREEN_HEIGHT, FPS, BLACK
# Initialize Pygame
pygame.init()
screen = pygame.display.set_mode((SCREEN_WIDTH, SCREEN_HEIGHT))
pygame.display.set_caption("RPG Game")
```

3.5 Adding Game States

RPGs often have different states, such as a main menu, gameplay, and game over screens. Let's set up a basic state manager:

1. Create a Game class in main.py:

python

Copy code

```
class Game:
    def init(self):
        self.running = True
    def run(self):
        clock = pygame.time.Clock()
        while self.running:
            self.handle_events()
            self.update()
            self.render()
            clock.tick(FPS)
    def handle_events(self):
        for event in pygame.event.get():
            if event.type == pygame.QUIT:
                self.running = False
    def update(self):
        pass  # Game logic goes
```

here def render(self): screen.fill(BLACK) # Clear the screen pygame.display.flip() # Update the display

2. Update the main() function:

python

Copy code

if name == "__main__": game = Game() game.run() pygame.quit() sys.exit()

3. Run the script. The game should still display a black screen, but now it's managed by the Game class.

3.6 Preparing for Sprites and Backgrounds

To add characters and backgrounds in the next chapters, we need to ensure our framework is ready to handle assets. Let's add placeholders for sprite groups and the background:

1. Update the Game class:

python

Copy code

def init(self): self.running = True self.all_sprites = pygame.sprite.Group() # Group for all game sprites def update(self): self.all_sprites.update() # Update all sprites def render(self): screen.fill(BLACK) self.all_sprites.draw(screen) # Draw all sprites pygame.display.flip()

2. Create a BaseSprite class in main.py for reusable sprite functionality:

```python
```

Copy code

```python
class BaseSprite(pygame.sprite.Sprite):
    def init(self, x, y, width, height, color):
        super().__init__()
        self.image = pygame.Surface((width, height))
        self.image.fill(color)
        self.rect = self.image.get_rect(topleft=(x, y))
```

3. Test the sprite system by adding a test sprite:

```python
```

Copy code

```python
def init(self):
    self.running = True
    self.all_sprites = pygame.sprite.Group()
    # Add a test sprite
    test_sprite = BaseSprite(100, 100, 50, 50, WHITE)
    self.all_sprites.add(test_sprite)
```

1. Run the game. A white square should appear on the screen.

Chapter 4: Programming Sprites

Sprites are essential elements in any RPG, representing characters, objects, or other interactive elements. In this chapter, you'll learn how to create and manage sprites for heroes, villains, and extra characters. We'll also add animations to bring them to life.

4.1 What Are Sprites?

A sprite is a 2D image or animation integrated into a larger scene. In RPGs, sprites are used for:

- Heroes: Player-controlled characters.
- Villains: Enemies with specific behaviors.

- Extras: Non-playable characters (NPCs) that add depth to the game world.

Pygame provides a robust Sprite class to handle these elements efficiently.

4.2 Creating a Base Sprite Class

To simplify the process, we'll create a reusable base class for sprites. This class will handle common functionality, such as rendering and movement.

1. Create a new file called character.py in the scripts/ folder.
2. Add the following code:

```python
Copy code

import pygame
class BaseSprite(pygame.sprite.Sprite):
    def init(self, x, y, width, height, color):
        super().__init__()
        self.image = pygame.Surface((width, height))
        self.image.fill(color)
        self.rect = self.image.get_rect(topleft=(x, y))
        self.velocity = pygame.math.Vector2(0, 0)
    def update(self):
        # Update the sprite's position based on velocity
        self.rect.x += self.velocity.x
        self.rect.y += self.velocity.y
```

This class provides:

- A visual representation (image and rect).
- Movement functionality using a velocity vector.

4.3 Creating the Hero Sprite

The hero sprite is the main character controlled by the player. Let's add movement functionality to it.

1. In character.py, create a Hero class:

    python

    Copy code

    ```python
    class Hero(BaseSprite):
        def __init__(self, x, y):
            super().__init__(x, y, 50, 50, (0, 255, 0))  # Green square for hero
        def handle_input(self, keys):
            self.velocity.x = 0
            self.velocity.y = 0
            if keys[pygame.K_UP]: self.velocity.y = -5
            if keys[pygame.K_DOWN]: self.velocity.y = 5
            if keys[pygame.K_LEFT]: self.velocity.x = -5
            if keys[pygame.K_RIGHT]: self.velocity.x = 5
    ```

2. In main.py, update the Game class to add the hero:

    python

    Copy code

    ```python
    from character import Hero
    class Game:
        def __init__(self):
            self.running = True
            self.all_sprites = pygame.sprite.Group()
            # Add the hero
            self.hero = Hero(100, 100)
            self.all_sprites.add(self.hero)
        def handle_events(self):
            keys = pygame.key.get_pressed()
            self.hero.handle_input(keys)
            for event in pygame.event.get():
                if event.type == pygame.QUIT:
                    self.running = False
    ```

3. Run the game. You should be able to move the green square (the hero) using the arrow keys.

4.4 Creating Villain Sprites

Villains are enemy characters that may move or perform actions. Let's create a simple villain with basic AI.

1. In character.py, create a Villain class:

   python

   Copy code

   ```
   import random
   class Villain(BaseSprite):
       def __init__(self, x, y):
           super().__init__(x, y, 50, 50, (255, 0, 0))  # Red square for villain
           self.direction = random.choice(['left', 'right', 'up', 'down'])

       def update(self):
           # Move the villain in a random direction
           if self.direction == 'left':
               self.velocity.x = -2
           elif self.direction == 'right':
               self.velocity.x = 2
           elif self.direction == 'up':
               self.velocity.y = -2
           elif self.direction == 'down':
               self.velocity.y = 2
           # Change direction randomly
           if random.randint(0, 100) < 2:
               self.direction = random.choice(['left', 'right', 'up', 'down'])
           super().update()
   ```

2. Add a villain to the game in main.py:

   python

   Copy code

   ```
   # Add a villain
   self.villain = Villain(300, 300)
   self.all_sprites.add(self.villain)
   ```

3. Run the game. The red square (villain) should move randomly around the screen.

4.5 Creating Extra Characters (NPCs)

NPCs are non-playable characters that might have interactions but don't actively move or fight.

1. In character.py, create an Extra class:

   python

   Copy code

   ```python
   class Extra(BaseSprite):
       def init(self, x, y, dialog):
           super().__init__(x, y, 40, 40, (0, 0, 255))  # Blue square for NPC
           self.dialog = dialog
       def talk(self):
           print(f"NPC says: {self.dialog}")
   ```

2. Add an NPC to the game in main.py:

   python

   Copy code

   ```python
   # Add an NPC
   self.npc = Extra(400, 200, "Welcome to the RPG world!")
   self.all_sprites.add(self.npc)
   ```

3. Update the handle_events method to allow interaction with NPCs:

   python

   Copy code

   ```python
   elif event.type == pygame.KEYDOWN and event.key == pygame.K_SPACE:
       if self.hero.rect.colliderect(self.npc.rect):
           self.npc.talk()
   ```

4. Run the game. Move the hero to the NPC and press the spacebar to trigger the dialog.

4.6 Animating Sprites

Let's animate the hero sprite by switching between different images.

1. Update the Hero class in character.py:

python

Copy code

```
class Hero(BaseSprite): def init(self, x, y): super().__init__(x, y, 50, 50, (0, 255, 0)) self.images = [pygame.image.load(f"assets/hero/frame_{i}.png") for i in range(1, 4)] self.image_index = 0 def update(self): # Update the animation self.image_index += 0.1 if self.image_index >= len(self.images): self.image_index = 0 self.image = self.images[int(self.image_index)] super().update()
```

2. Add three hero images (frame_1.png, frame_2.png, frame_3.png) to the assets/hero/ folder.
3. Run the game. The hero should now have a walking animation.

Chapter 5: Programming the Background

The background is the foundation of your game world, providing visual context and immersing players in the RPG environment. In this chapter, you'll learn how to create and manage static backgrounds, scrolling backgrounds, and tile-based backgrounds.

5.1 Understanding Backgrounds in Games

Backgrounds in RPGs serve multiple purposes:

- Visual Depth: Provides context for the game's setting (e.g., forests, cities, dungeons).
- Interactivity: Some backgrounds have interactive elements, like doors or obstacles.

- Navigation: Guides the player on where they can move or explore.

Pygame allows us to load and manipulate images, making it easy to create dynamic and interactive backgrounds.

5.2 Loading a Static Background

A static background doesn't change as the player moves. This is suitable for small game areas.

1. Add a background image to the assets/backgrounds/ folder (e.g., background.png).

2. Update background.py in the scripts/ folder:

    python

    Copy code

    import pygame class StaticBackground: def init(self, image_path, screen): self.image = pygame.image.load(image_path) self.screen = screen def draw(self): self.screen.blit(self.image, (0, 0))

3. Integrate the static background into the game in main.py:

    python

    Copy code

    from background import StaticBackground class Game: def init(self): self.running = True self.all_sprites = pygame.sprite.Group() # Add a static background self.background = StaticBackground("assets/backgrounds/background.png",

screen) # Add the hero self.hero = Hero(100, 100)
self.all_sprites.add(self.hero) def render(self):
self.background.draw() # Draw the background
self.all_sprites.draw(screen) # Draw sprites
pygame.display.flip() # Update the display

4. Run the game. You should see a background image behind the sprites.

5.3 Adding a Scrolling Background

A scrolling background creates the illusion of movement, often used in games with large maps.

1. Update background.py to include a scrolling background class:

    python

    Copy code

    class ScrollingBackground: def init(self, image_path, screen, speed): self.image = pygame.image.load(image_path) self.screen = screen self.speed = speed self.offset = 0 def update(self): self.offset += self.speed if self.offset >= self.image.get_width(): self.offset = 0 def draw(self): self.screen.blit(self.image, (-self.offset, 0)) self.screen.blit(self.image, (self.image.get_width() - self.offset, 0))

2. Replace the static background with the scrolling background in main.py:

    python

    Copy code

```
self.background =
ScrollingBackground("assets/backgrounds/scrolling_background.png", screen, speed=2)
```

1. Update the game loop to include the background's update() method:

```python
```

Copy code

```
def update(self):
    self.background.update()  # Update background scrolling
    self.all_sprites.update()  # Update sprites
```

2. Run the game. The background should now scroll horizontally, creating a sense of motion.

5.4 Creating a Tile-Based Background

Tile-based backgrounds are modular and consist of repeated tiles to form a larger map. This is useful for RPGs with large, interactive worlds.

1. Create a tilemap image set (e.g., tileset.png) and save it in assets/backgrounds/.

2. Update background.py to include a TileMap class:

```python
```

Copy code

```
class TileMap:
    def __init__(self, tileset_path, tile_size, map_data, screen):
        self.tileset = pygame.image.load(tileset_path)
        self.tile_size = tile_size
        self.map_data = map_data
        self.screen
```

= screen self.tiles = self._load_tiles() def loadtiles(self): tiles = [] tileset_width = self.tileset.get_width() // self.tile_size tileset_height = self.tileset.get_height() // self.tile_size for y in range(tileset_height): for x in range(tileset_width): rect = pygame.Rect(x self.tile_size, y self.tile_size, self.tile_size, self.tile_size) tiles.append(self.tileset.subsurface(rect)) return tiles def draw(self): for row_idx, row in enumerate(self.map_data): for col_idx, tile_id in enumerate(row): if tile_id >= 0: x, y = col_idx self.tile_size, row_idx self.tile_size self.screen.blit(self.tiles[tile_id], (x, y))

1. Create a sample tilemap in main.py:

   python

   Copy code

   # Sample tilemap (0: grass, 1: water, -1: empty) tilemap_data = [[0, 0, 0, 1, 1, 1], [0, 0, 0, 1, 1, 1], [0, 0, 0, 1, 1, 1], [0, 0, 0, 0, 0, 0]] self.background = TileMap("assets/backgrounds/tileset.png", tile_size=32, map_data=tilemap_data, screen=screen)

2. Replace the draw() method in the Game class to draw the tilemap:

   python

   Copy code

   self.background.draw() # Draw the tilemap
   self.all_sprites.draw(screen) # Draw sprites
   pygame.display.flip() # Update the display

3. Run the game. You should see a tile-based background rendered on the screen.

5.5 Adding Interactivity to Backgrounds

Interactive backgrounds allow players to interact with objects, like opening doors or triggering events.

1. Update TileMap to include interaction logic:

    python

    Copy code

    ```
    def get_tile_at(self, x, y): col, row = x // self.tile_size, y // self.tile_size if 0 <= row < len(self.map_data) and 0 <= col < len(self.map_data[row]): return self.map_data[row][col] return -1
    ```

2. Check interactions in main.py:

    python

    Copy code

    ```
    elif event.type == pygame.KEYDOWN and event.key == pygame.K_SPACE: tile_id = self.background.get_tile_at(self.hero.rect.x, self.hero.rect.y) if tile_id == 1: # Example: 1 represents water print("You stepped into water!")
    ```

3. Run the game. Move the hero over different tiles and press the spacebar to trigger interactions.

By the end of this chapter, you have created static, scrolling, and tile-based backgrounds and added interactivity to enhance your RPG's world. In the next chapter, we'll focus on gameplay elements like collision detection and combat mechanics!

Chapter 6: Adding Gameplay Elements

Gameplay mechanics are the heart of an RPG, providing the player with interactive features and challenges. In this chapter, you'll implement key gameplay elements, including movement boundaries, collision detection, health systems, and combat mechanics.

6.1 Adding Movement Boundaries

To prevent the player from moving off-screen, we need to define boundaries for the hero sprite.

1. Update the Hero class in character.py:

    python

    Copy code

    ```
    class Hero(BaseSprite): def init(self, x, y): super().__init__(x, y, 50, 50, (0, 255, 0)) # Green square for hero def handle_input(self, keys): self.velocity.x = 0 self.velocity.y = 0 if keys[pygame.K_UP]: self.velocity.y = -5 if keys[pygame.K_DOWN]: self.velocity.y = 5 if keys[pygame.K_LEFT]: self.velocity.x = -5 if keys[pygame.K_RIGHT]: self.velocity.x = 5 def update(self): # Update the position super().update() # Constrain the hero to screen boundaries if self.rect.left < 0: self.rect.left = 0 if self.rect.right > SCREEN_WIDTH: self.rect.right = SCREEN_WIDTH if self.rect.top < 0: self.rect.top = 0 if self.rect.bottom > SCREEN_HEIGHT: self.rect.bottom = SCREEN_HEIGHT
    ```

2. Test the game by trying to move the hero beyond the screen edges. The sprite should now stay within bounds.

6.2 Collision Detection

Collision detection allows characters to interact with objects and obstacles in the game world. Let's enable the hero to collide with villains.

1. Add collision detection to the update() method of the Game class in main.py:

python

Copy code

def update(self): self.background.update() # Update background scrolling self.all_sprites.update() # Update sprites # Check collision between hero and villain if pygame.sprite.collide_rect(self.hero, self.villain): print("Collision detected!")

2. Run the game. When the hero overlaps the villain, "Collision detected!" will print in the console.

6.3 Adding a Health System

Health systems allow the hero and villains to take damage. Let's add health attributes and display them on the screen.

1. Update the Hero and Villain classes in character.py:

python

Copy code

class Hero(BaseSprite): def init(self, x, y): super().__init__(x, y, 50, 50, (0, 255, 0)) self.health = 100 class Villain(BaseSprite): def init(self, x, y): super().__init__(x, y, 50, 50, (255, 0, 0)) self.health = 50

2. Add a method to render health bars in main.py:

   python

   Copy code

   ```
   def render_health_bar(self, entity):
       pygame.draw.rect(screen, (255, 0, 0), (entity.rect.x, entity.rect.y - 10, 50, 5))  # Background
       pygame.draw.rect(screen, (0, 255, 0), (entity.rect.x, entity.rect.y - 10, max(0, entity.health / 2), 5))  # Health
   ```

1. Update the render() method to draw health bars:

   python

   Copy code

   ```
   self.background.draw()  # Draw the background
   self.all_sprites.draw(screen)  # Draw sprites
   # Draw health bars
   self.render_health_bar(self.hero)
   self.render_health_bar(self.villain)
   pygame.display.flip()  # Update the display
   ```

2. Run the game. Health bars should now appear above the hero and villain.

6.4 Implementing Combat Mechanics

Combat mechanics allow the hero and villain to interact through attacks and damage.

1. Add an attack() method to the Hero and Villain classes in character.py:

   python

Copy code

```python
class Hero(BaseSprite):
    def attack(self, target):
        target.health -= 10
        print(f"Hero attacked! Villain's health: {target.health}")

class Villain(BaseSprite):
    def attack(self, target):
        target.health -= 5
        print(f"Villain attacked! Hero's health: {target.health}")
```

2. Enable the hero to attack the villain by pressing the spacebar in main.py:

python

Copy code

```python
elif event.type == pygame.KEYDOWN and event.key == pygame.K_SPACE:
    if pygame.sprite.collide_rect(self.hero, self.villain):
        self.hero.attack(self.villain)
```

3. Run the game. Move the hero to collide with the villain and press the spacebar to attack.

6.5 Handling Defeat

When a character's health reaches zero, they are removed from the game.

1. Update the update() method in Game to handle defeat:

python

Copy code

```python
if self.villain.health <= 0:
    self.all_sprites.remove(self.villain)
    print("Villain defeated!")
if self.hero.health <= 0:
    print("Game Over! Hero defeated!")
    self.running = False
```

2. Test the game by attacking the villain until their health reaches zero.

6.6 Adding Score and Inventory Systems

RPGs often include scores and inventories to track progress.

1. Add a score attribute to the Game class:

    python

    Copy code

    ```
    self.score = 0
    ```

2. Update the Hero attack method to increase the score when the villain is defeated:

    python

    Copy code

    ```
    def attack(self, target): target.health -= 10 if target.health <= 0: game.score += 100 print(f"Villain defeated! Score: {game.score}")
    ```

3. Add an inventory system to the Hero class:

    python

    Copy code

    ```
    class Hero(BaseSprite): def init(self, x, y): super().__init__(x, y, 50, 50, (0, 255, 0)) self.health = 100 self.inventory = [] def collect_item(self, item): self.inventory.append(item) print(f"Collected: {item}")
    ```

1. Add items to the game and enable the hero to collect them:

   python

   Copy code

   ```python
   class Item(BaseSprite):
       def init(self, x, y, name):
           super().__init__(x, y, 20, 20, (255, 255, 0))  # Yellow square
           self.name = name
   self.item = Item(400, 300, "Magic Potion")
   self.all_sprites.add(self.item)
   if pygame.sprite.collide_rect(self.hero, self.item):
       self.hero.collect_item(self.item.name)
       self.all_sprites.remove(self.item)
   ```

2. Run the game. The hero should now collect items and gain points by defeating villains.

By the end of this chapter, your game will have core gameplay mechanics, including movement boundaries, collision detection, combat, health systems, and item collection. In the next chapter, we'll add visual and audio enhancements to bring your RPG to life!

Chapter 7: Enhancing Visuals and Audio

Adding engaging visuals and audio can significantly elevate the quality of your RPG, making it more immersive and enjoyable. In this chapter, we'll focus on improving the game's presentation by incorporating animations, sound effects, and background music.

7.1 Improving Sprite Animations

Animations bring life to characters and objects in your game. We'll use sprite sheets to add animations for movement, attacks, and idle states.

1. Create a Sprite Sheet:

- Prepare a sprite sheet with frames for your character's actions (e.g., walking, attacking).
- Save the sprite sheet as hero_spritesheet.png in the assets/characters/ folder.

2. Update the Hero Class: Add animation handling to the Hero class in character.py:

python

Copy code

```
class Hero(BaseSprite):
    def init(self, x, y):
        super().__init__(x, y, 50, 50, (0, 255, 0))
        self.spritesheet = pygame.image.load("assets/characters/hero_spritesheet.png")
        self.frames = self._load_frames()
        self.current_frame = 0
        self.frame_delay = 5
        self.frame_counter = 0
    def loadframes(self):
        frames = []
        for i in range(4):  # Assuming 4 frames for walking
            frame = self.spritesheet.subsurface(pygame.Rect(i * 50, 0, 50, 50))
            frames.append(frame)
        return frames
    def update(self):
        self.frame_counter += 1
        if self.frame_counter >= self.frame_delay:
            self.frame_counter = 0
            self.current_frame = (self.current_frame + 1) % len(self.frames)
            self.image = self.frames[self.current_frame]
        super().update()
```

3. Run the game. The hero should now animate as they move.

7.2 Adding Background Music

Background music creates atmosphere and sets the tone for your game.

1. Add a music file (e.g., background_music.mp3) to the assets/sounds/ folder.

2. Update main.py to include music playback:

```python
```

Copy code

```
import pygame.mixer
class Game:
    def init(self):
        self.running = True
        pygame.mixer.init()
        pygame.mixer.music.load("assets/sounds/background_music.mp3")
        pygame.mixer.music.play(-1)  # Loop indefinitely
```

3. Run the game. You should hear the background music playing.

7.3 Incorporating Sound Effects

Sound effects make interactions more engaging, such as when characters attack or collect items.

1. Add sound effect files (e.g., attack.wav and collect_item.wav) to the assets/sounds/ folder.

2. Update the Hero class to include sound effects:

```python
```

Copy code

```
class Hero(BaseSprite):
    def init(self, x, y):
        super().__init__(x, y, 50, 50, (0, 255, 0))
        self.attack_sound = pygame.mixer.Sound("assets/sounds/attack.wav")
        self.collect_sound = pygame.mixer.Sound("assets/sounds/collect_item.wav")
    def attack(self, target):
        self.attack_sound.play()
        target.health -= 10
    def collect_item(self, item):
        self.collect_sound.play()
        self.inventory.append(item)
        print(f"Collected: {item}")
```

3. Run the game. When the hero attacks or collects items, you should hear the corresponding sound effects.

7.4 Creating Visual Effects

Visual effects, such as explosions or spell animations, make gameplay more dynamic.

1. Add an explosion effect in character.py:

    python

    Copy code

    ```python
    class Explosion(BaseSprite):
        def init(self, x, y):
            super().__init__(x, y, 50, 50, (255, 0, 0))
            self.spritesheet = pygame.image.load("assets/effects/explosion_spritesheet.png")
            self.frames = self._load_frames()
            self.current_frame = 0
            self.frame_delay = 3
            self.frame_counter = 0
            self.animation_done = False

        def loadframes(self):
            frames = []
            for i in range(4):  # Assuming 4 frames for explosion
                frame = self.spritesheet.subsurface(pygame.Rect(i * 50, 0, 50, 50))
                frames.append(frame)
            return frames

        def update(self):
            self.frame_counter += 1
            if self.frame_counter >= self.frame_delay:
                self.frame_counter = 0
                self.current_frame += 1
                if self.current_frame >= len(self.frames):
                    self.animation_done = True
                    self.kill()  # Remove explosion from the sprite group
                else:
                    self.image = self.frames[self.current_frame]
    ```

2. Add explosions during combat in main.py:

    python

    Copy code

    ```python
    if pygame.sprite.collide_rect(self.hero, self.villain):
        self.hero.attack(self.villain)
        explosion = Explosion(self.villain.rect.x, self.villain.rect.y)
        self.all_sprites.add(explosion)
    ```

3. Run the game. When the hero attacks, an explosion effect should appear.

7.5 Adding Particle Effects

Particle effects like sparkles, rain, or fireflies can add extra polish to your game.

1. Add a Particle class in character.py:

   python

   Copy code

   ```
   import random
   class Particle(pygame.sprite.Sprite):
       def __init__(self, x, y, color, lifetime):
           super().__init__()
           self.image = pygame.Surface((5, 5))
           self.image.fill(color)
           self.rect = self.image.get_rect(center=(x, y))
           self.lifetime = lifetime
           self.velocity = pygame.math.Vector2(random.uniform(-2, 2), random.uniform(-2, 2))
       def update(self):
           self.rect.x += self.velocity.x
           self.rect.y += self.velocity.y
           self.lifetime -= 1
           if self.lifetime <= 0:
               self.kill()
   ```

2. Add particles during interactions, such as when collecting items:

   python

   Copy code

   ```
   for _ in range(10):  # Create 10 particles
       particle = Particle(self.item.rect.x, self.item.rect.y, (255, 255, 0), lifetime=30)
       self.allsprites.add(particle)
   ```

3. Run the game. When the hero collects an item, a burst of particles should appear.

35

7.6 Polishing the User Interface

A polished user interface improves player experience. Let's add a score display.

1. Add a draw_score method in main.py:

    python

    Copy code

    ```python
    def draw_score(self): font = pygame.font.Font(None, 36) score_text = font.render(f"Score: {self.score}", True, (255, 255, 255)) screen.blit(score_text, (10, 10))
    ```

2. Update the render() method to include the score:

    python

    Copy code

    ```python
    self.background.draw() # Draw the background self.all_sprites.draw(screen) # Draw sprites self.draw_score() # Draw the score pygame.display.flip() # Update the display
    ```

3. Run the game. The current score should appear in the top-left corner.

By the end of this chapter, your game should feature smooth animations, engaging sound effects, immersive background music, and polished visual elements. These enhancements will make your RPG look and feel professional. In the next chapter, we'll implement saving and loading game progress!

Chapter 8: Saving and Loading Progress

Saving and loading game progress is a crucial feature for any RPG, allowing players to resume their adventures from where they left off. In this chapter, we'll implement systems to save game state (e.g., hero attributes, inventory, and position) and load it when the game restarts.

8.1 Understanding Game State

The game state represents the current status of your game, including:

- Hero attributes: Health, position, and inventory.
- Villain and NPC statuses: Positions, health, and whether they've been defeated.
- Score: The current game score.
- Environment: The state of items, tiles, or other interactive elements.

We'll save this data in a JSON file for easy storage and retrieval.

8.2 Saving the Game

1. Create a Save Function: In main.py, add a method to save the game state:

python

Copy code

```
import json class Game: def init(self): self.running = True self.score = 0 self.hero = Hero(100, 100) self.all_sprites = pygame.sprite.Group() self.all_sprites.add(self.hero) def save_game(self): save_data = { "hero": { "x": self.hero.rect.x, "y": self.hero.rect.y, "health": self.hero.health, "inventory": self.hero.inventory, }, "score": self.score, } with open("save_game.json", "w") as save_file: json.dump(save_data, save_file) print("Game saved!")
```

37

2. **Trigger the Save Function:** Add a keybinding to save the game:

    python

    Copy code

    ```
    for event in pygame.event.get():
        if event.type == pygame.KEYDOWN:
            if event.key == pygame.K_s:  # Press 'S' to save
                self.save_game()
    ```

3. **Test the game:**
    - Move the hero or collect items.
    - Press S to save the game.
    - Check that save_game.json contains the correct data.

8.3 Loading the Game

1. **Create a Load Function:** In main.py, add a method to load the game state:

    python

    Copy code

    ```
    def load_game(self):
        try:
            with open("save_game.json", "r") as save_file:
                save_data = json.load(save_file)
                # Restore hero attributes
                self.hero.rect.x = save_data["hero"]["x"]
                self.hero.rect.y = save_data["hero"]["y"]
                self.hero.health = save_data["hero"]["health"]
                self.hero.inventory = save_data["hero"]["inventory"]
                # Restore score
                self.score = save_data["score"]
                print("Game loaded!")
        except FileNotFoundError:
            print("No save file found!")
    ```

2. **Trigger the Load Function**: Add a keybinding to load the game:

python

Copy code

if event.type == pygame.KEYDOWN: if event.key == pygame.K_l: # Press 'L' to load self.load_game()

3. **Test the game**:

    - Save the game.
    - Restart the game and press L to load the saved progress.

8.4 Saving and Loading NPCs, Villains, and Items

To make the save system comprehensive, include other game elements like villains and items.

1. **Extend the Save Function**: Update save_game to include villains and items:

python

Copy code

save_data["villains"] = [{"x": villain.rect.x, "y": villain.rect.y, "health": <u>villain.health</u>} for villain in self.all_sprites if isinstance(villain, Villain)]
save_data["items"] = [{"x": item.rect.x, "y": item.rect.y, "name": <u>item.name</u>} for item in self.all_sprites if isinstance(item, Item)]

2. Extend the Load Function: Update load_game to restore villains and items:

python

Copy code

for villain_data in save_data.get("villains", []): villain = Villain(villain_data["x"], villain_data["y"]) villain.health = villain_data["health"] self.all_sprites.add(villain) for item_data in save_data.get("items", []): item = Item(item_data["x"], item_data["y"], item_data["name"]) self.all_sprites.add(item)

3. Test the game:

    o Save the game when villains and items are on screen.
    o Restart and load the game. Villains and items should reappear in their saved states.

8.5 Autosaving

Autosaving ensures that progress isn't lost unexpectedly.

1. Implement Autosaving: Add autosave functionality in the game loop:

python

Copy code

autosave_counter = 0 while self.running: autosave_counter += 1 if autosave_counter >= 600: # Autosave every 10 seconds (600 frames at 60 FPS) self.save_game() autosave_counter = 0

2. Test the game:

    - Play for a while without saving manually.
    - Restart and load the game. The autosave file should reflect recent progress.

8.6 Adding a Save/Load Menu

A menu makes saving and loading more user-friendly.

1. Create a Menu State: Add a menu_active flag to the Game class:

python

Copy code

self.menu_active = False

2. Render the Menu: Create a render_menu method:

python

Copy code

def render_menu(self): font = pygame.font.Font(None, 36) save_text = font.render("Press S to Save", True, (255, 255, 255)) load_text = font.render("Press L to Load", True, (255, 255, 255)) screen.blit(save_text, (SCREEN_WIDTH // 2 - 100, SCREEN_HEIGHT // 2 - 50)) screen.blit(load_text, (SCREEN_WIDTH // 2 - 100, SCREEN_HEIGHT // 2)) pygame.display.flip()

3. Toggle the Menu: Add a keybinding to toggle the menu:

```python
```

Copy code

```
elif event.type == pygame.KEYDOWN and event.key == pygame.K_m:  # Press 'M' for menu
    self.menu_active = not self.menu_active
```

1. Integrate the Menu into the Game Loop: Update the game loop to handle the menu:

```python
```

Copy code

```
while self.running:
    if self.menu_active:
        self.render_menu()
        continue
    self.handle_events()
    self.update()
    self.render()
```

2. Test the game:
   - Press M to open the menu.
   - Use the menu to save and load the game.

8.7 Enhancing the Save/Load System

For more polished functionality:

- Confirmations: Add pop-ups to confirm saves/loads.
- Multiple Save Slots: Use multiple JSON files (e.g., save_slot_1.json, save_slot_2.json).
- Timestamps: Save the date and time of each save.

By the end of this chapter, your game will support saving and loading progress, allowing players to resume their adventures seamlessly. In the next chapter, we'll explore how to expand the game by adding new levels, quests, and features!

Chapter 9: Expanding the Game

Once the core mechanics of your RPG are in place, it's time to expand the game world. In this chapter, we'll explore how to add new levels, quests, and features to make your RPG more engaging and scalable.

9.1 Adding Multiple Levels

Levels provide progression and variety in gameplay. Let's implement a system to transition between levels.

1. Level Data Structure: Create level configurations in a levels.py file:

    ```python
    ```

    Copy code

    ```
    level_data = [ { "background": "assets/backgrounds/level1.png", "villains": [ {"x": 300, "y": 300, "health": 50}, {"x": 500, "y": 200, "health": 50}, ], "items": [ {"x": 400, "y": 400, "name": "Health Potion"}, ], }, { "background": "assets/backgrounds/level2.png", "villains": [ {"x": 200, "y": 300, "health": 70}, {"x": 600, "y": 100, "health": 70}, ], "items": [ {"x": 350, "y": 250, "name": "Mana Potion"}, ], }, ]
    ```

2. Level Transition System: Add level transitions in the Game class:

    ```python
    ```

    Copy code

```python
from levels import level_data
class Game:
    def init(self):
        self.running = True
        self.current_level = 0
        self.load_level(self.current_level)
    def load_level(self, level_index):
        level = level_data[level_index]
        self.background = StaticBackground(level["background"], screen)
        self.all_sprites.empty()
        # Add villains
        for villain_info in level["villains"]:
            villain = Villain(villain_info["x"], villain_info["y"])
            villain.health = villain_info["health"]
            self.all_sprites.add(villain)
        # Add items
        for item_info in level["items"]:
            item = Item(item_info["x"], item_info["y"], item_info["name"])
            self.all_sprites.add(item)
        # Add hero
        self.hero = Hero(100, 100)
        self.all_sprites.add(self.hero)
```

1. Transition to the Next Level: Transition when all villains are defeated:

python

Copy code

```python
def update(self):
    self.background.update()
    self.all_sprites.update()
    # Check if all villains are defeated
    villains = [sprite for sprite in self.all_sprites if isinstance(sprite, Villain)]
    if not villains and self.current_level < len(level_data) - 1:
        self.current_level += 1
        self.load_level(self.current_level)
        print(f"Level {self.current_level + 1} loaded!")
```

2. Test the game:

Defeat all villains in a level to progress to the next one.

9.2 Adding Quests

Quests give players goals and create an immersive storyline.

1. **Quest System:** Add a Quest class in <u>quests.py</u>:

   python

   Copy code

   ```python
   class Quest:
       def __init__(self, description, goal, reward):
           self.description = description
           self.goal = goal
           self.reward = reward
           self.completed = False

       def check_completion(self, player):
           if self.goal(player):
               self.completed = True
               print(f"Quest Complete! Reward: {self.reward}")
               return True
           return False
   ```

2. **Assign Quests:** Add a quest to the game:

   python

   Copy code

   ```python
   from quests import Quest

   def villain_defeat_goal(player):
       return player.score >= 100

   class Game:
       def __init__(self):
           self.running = True
           self.quests = [
               Quest("Defeat 2 villains to earn a reward.", villain_defeat_goal, "Golden Sword")
           ]

       def update(self):
           for quest in self.quests:
               if not quest.completed:
                   quest.check_completion(self.hero)
   ```

3. **Test the game:**

   Defeat villains to complete the quest and earn the reward.

9.3 Expanding the World

Expand the game world by adding larger maps or areas to explore.

1. **Scrolling Maps:** Update the Hero class to move the background when near the screen edges:

python

Copy code

```
def update(self): if self.rect.right > SCREEN_WIDTH - 50: self.rect.right = SCREEN_WIDTH - 50 self.move_background(-5, 0) elif self.rect.left < 50: self.rect.left = 50 self.move_background(5, 0)
```

Add move_background to shift the map:

python

Copy code

```
def move_background(self, dx, dy): self.background.offset_x += dx self.background.offset_y += dy
```

9.4 Adding Dialog

NPC dialog deepens the narrative and guides players through quests.

1. Add Dialog to NPCs: Update the Extra class to include dialog options:

   python

   Copy code

   ```
   class Extra(BaseSprite): def init(self, x, y, dialog): super().__init__(x, y, 40, 40, (0, 0, 255)) self.dialog = dialog def talk(self): print(f"NPC says: {self.dialog}")
   ```

2. Trigger dialog when the hero interacts with NPCs:

```python
```
Copy code

```python
if pygame.sprite.collide_rect(self.hero, self.npc):
    self.npc.talk()
```

3. Test the game:

Add NPCs with different dialog and interact with them.

9.5 Enhancing Replayability

Replayability ensures players keep coming back to your game.

1. Randomized Levels: Randomize villain and item positions:

```python
```
Copy code

```python
import random
villain_info["x"] = random.randint(100, SCREEN_WIDTH - 100)
villain_info["y"] = random.randint(100, SCREEN_HEIGHT - 100)
```

2. Difficulty Scaling: Increase villain health and number as the levels progress:

```python
```
Copy code

```python
villain.health += self.current_level * 10
```

1. Achievements: Add an achievement system for milestones:

```python
```

Copy code

```python
class Achievement:
    def init(self, description, condition):
        self.description = description
        self.condition = condition
        self.unlocked = False
    def check_unlock(self, player):
        if self.condition(player) and not self.unlocked:
            self.unlocked = True
            print(f"Achievement Unlocked: {self.description}")
```

Example achievement:

```python
```

Copy code

```python
Achievement("First Blood: Defeat your first villain.", lambda player: player.score >= 50)
```

9.6 Adding Customization

1. Hero Customization: Let players choose hero colors or sprite:

   ```python
   ```

   Copy code

   ```python
   hero_color = (0, 255, 0) if input("Choose Green (G) or Red (R): ").lower() == "g" else (255, 0, 0)
   self.hero = Hero(100, 100, hero_color)
   ```

2. Skill Trees: Add a skill upgrade system:

   ```python
   ```

   Copy code

```
class SkillTree: def init(self): self.skills = {"Strength": 0,
"Speed": 0} def upgrade(self, skill): if skill in self.skills:
self.skills[skill] += 1 print(f"{skill} upgraded to level
{self.skills[skill]}")
```

Integrate into the hero:

python

Copy code

```
self.hero.skills.upgrade("Strength")
```

By the end of this chapter, your RPG will feature multiple levels, quests, dialog, and customization options. These expansions will make your game richer, more engaging, and replayable. In the next chapter, we'll cover how to polish and release your game!

Chapter 10: Polishing and Releasing Your RPG

Congratulations! You've built a functional RPG with exciting gameplay mechanics and features. In this chapter, we'll focus on polishing your game, preparing it for release, and making it available for others to play.

10.1 Optimizing Performance

Optimizing your game ensures it runs smoothly on different devices.

1. Optimize Asset Sizes:

    - Compress images and audio files to reduce file size.
    - Use online tools like TinyPNG for images.
    - Convert audio files to lower bitrates (e.g., 128 kbps).

2. Efficient Sprite Management: Use sprite groups effectively to avoid unnecessary rendering:

python

Copy code

```
visible_sprites = pygame.sprite.Group() for sprite in self.all_sprites: if sprite.rect.colliderect(screen.get_rect()): visible_sprites.add(sprite) visible_sprites.draw(screen)
```

3. Limit FPS: Cap the frame rate to reduce CPU usage:

python

Copy code

```
clock.tick(60) # Limit to 60 FPS
```

4. Optimize Collision Detection: Use Pygame's spritecollide or collide_mask for efficient collision checks.

10.2 Polishing Visuals

1. Add a Title Screen: Create a TitleScreen class:

python

Copy code

```
class TitleScreen: def init(self): self.active = True def display(self): font = pygame.font.Font(None, 72) title_text = font.render("RPG Adventure", True, (255, 255, 255)) screen.blit(title_text, (SCREEN_WIDTH // 2 - 200, SCREEN_HEIGHT // 2 - 50)) pygame.display.flip() def handle_events(self): for event in pygame.event.get(): if
```

event.type == pygame.KEYDOWN: if event.key == pygame.K_RETURN: # Start the game on Enter self.active = False

Display the title screen in main.py:

```python
```

Copy code

title_screen = TitleScreen() while title_screen.active: title_screen.handle_events() title_screen.display()

1. Add Transition Effects: Fade in and out between levels:

```python
```

Copy code

def fade_screen(color, duration): fade_surface = pygame.Surface(screen.get_size()) fade_surface.fill(color) for alpha in range(0, 255, duration): fade_surface.set_alpha(alpha) screen.blit(fade_surface, (0, 0)) pygame.display.flip() clock.tick(60)

2. Add Particle Effects: Use particle systems for environmental effects like rain, snow, or sparkles.

10.3 Enhancing Audio

1. Dynamic Background Music: Change music based on game events or levels:

```python
```

Copy code

```
def change_music(track):
pygame.mixer.music.fadeout(1000) # Fade out current music
pygame.mixer.music.load(track) pygame.mixer.music.play(-1)
```

2. **Spatial Sound Effects**: Adjust sound volume based on the hero's proximity to the source:

python

Copy code

```
def adjust_sound_volume(entity, listener): distance = pygame.math.Vector2(entity.rect.center).distance_to(listener.rect.center) volume = max(0, 1 - (distance / 500)) # Scale volume entity.sound.set_volume(volume)
```

10.4 Testing Your Game

1. **Playtesting**: Recruit friends or beta testers to play your game and provide feedback.

    - Observe where players struggle or lose interest.
    - Use feedback to tweak game balance, level design, or UI.

2. **Debugging Tools**: Use PyCharm's debugging features to track and fix bugs:

    - Set breakpoints in critical sections of your code.
    - Log gameplay events to identify unexpected behaviors.

3. **Edge Case Testing**: Test extreme cases like:

    - Moving the hero to every corner of the map.

- Saving and loading with unusual data.
- Performing actions at unexpected times (e.g., during transitions).

10.5 Preparing for Release

1. **Package Your Game:** Use pyinstaller to bundle your game into an executable:

```bash
Copy code

pip install pyinstaller
pyinstaller --onefile --windowed main.py
```

- --onefile: Packages everything into a single executable.
- --windowed: Removes the console window.

The executable will be located in the dist/ folder.

2. **Create an Icon:** Add a custom icon to your game:

- Save your icon as game_icon.ico.
- Add the --icon=game_icon.ico flag to the pyinstaller command.

3. **Write Documentation:** Include a README.txt file with:

- A brief description of the game.
- Controls and instructions.
- Minimum system requirements.

4. **Distribute Your Game:**

- Share your game on platforms like Itch.io, GameJolt, or your own website.
- Compress your game files into a .zip or .exe installer.

10.6 Promoting Your Game

1. Create a Trailer:

    - Record gameplay using tools like OBS Studio.
    - Edit the video to highlight exciting features.
2. Social Media: Share screenshots, trailers, and development updates on platforms like Twitter, Instagram, and Reddit.
3. Community Engagement: Post about your game in relevant forums and communities (e.g., r/IndieDev on Reddit).
4. Feedback Loop: Encourage players to leave reviews or report bugs. Use this feedback to release updates and improve the game.

10.7 Future Expansion

1. DLC or Updates:

    - Add new levels, characters, or quests after release.
    - Release updates to fix bugs or add requested features.

2. Monetization:

    - If you plan to sell the game, set up a payment system through platforms like Itch.io or Steam.
    - Consider adding optional in-game purchases like skins or bonus content.
3. Open Source: Share your game's source code on platforms like GitHub to allow others to learn from or contribute to your project.

10.8 Conclusion

You've taken your RPG from concept to a polished, distributable game. With engaging gameplay, immersive visuals, and thoughtful design, your project has the potential to captivate players and showcase your skills as a developer. Remember, game development is an iterative process—continue refining, expanding, and learning from each project you create.

Now it's time to release your RPG to the world and start your journey as a game developer!

Chapter 11: Learning and Growing as a Game Developer

Completing your RPG is a significant milestone, but it's only the beginning of your journey as a game developer. This chapter focuses on refining your skills, exploring advanced concepts, and building a portfolio to showcase your work.

11.1 Reflecting on Your Project

1. What Went Well:

   - Identify features or mechanics you're particularly proud of.
   - Reflect on how your planning and execution aligned with your initial goals.

2. Areas for Improvement:

   - Note challenges you faced during development.
   - Consider how you can address these challenges in future projects.

3. Lessons Learned:

- Document the key takeaways from your development experience.
- Example: "Efficient project organization saved time during debugging."

11.2 Expanding Your Skills

1. Explore Advanced Game Development Concepts:

    - Artificial Intelligence (AI):
        - Create more intelligent NPCs and enemies using pathfinding algorithms like A*.
        - Implement behavior trees for dynamic decision-making.

    - Procedural Generation:
        - Use algorithms to generate random maps, levels, or quests.
        - Example: Procedural dungeons with unique layouts each playthrough.

    - Physics:

    Integrate realistic physics for movement, collisions, or special effects.

2. Learn Other Game Development Frameworks:

    - Try alternatives to Pygame, such as:
        - Godot Engine: Lightweight and beginner-friendly.
        - Unity: Industry-standard for 2D and 3D games (C# required).

- Unreal Engine: Powerful for 3D games (uses Blueprints or C++).

1. Enhance Your Python Knowledge:

    o Dive deeper into Python concepts:

    - Object-Oriented Programming (OOP) design patterns.
    - Advanced data structures for optimized performance.
    - Using Python libraries for networking (e.g., socket for multiplayer games).

2. Master Game Art and Audio:

    o Learn tools for creating custom assets:

    - Art: Tools like Aseprite, GIMP, or Photoshop for pixel art.
    - Audio: Tools like Audacity or FL Studio for sound effects and music.

11.3 Building a Portfolio

A portfolio showcases your skills and attracts potential employers, collaborators, or clients.

1. Showcase Your RPG:

    o Include screenshots, gameplay videos, and descriptions.
    o Highlight the unique features of your game.

2. Host Your Work Online:

- Create a website or portfolio on platforms like:
    - GitHub Pages: Free hosting for code and projects.
    - Itch.io: Share your games with a community of developers and players.
    - ArtStation/Behance: Showcase game art or design work.

3. Document Your Process:

    - Write blog posts or tutorials about your development process.
    - Include lessons learned, challenges faced, and solutions implemented.

11.4 Networking in the Game Development Community

1. Join Online Communities:

    - Participate in forums like:
        - Reddit: r/IndieDev, r/GameDev, r/Python.
        - Discord: Join servers dedicated to game development and programming.
        - Stack Overflow: Ask questions and help others solve problems.

2. Contribute to Open Source Projects:

    - Collaborate on GitHub projects related to game development.
    - Build your reputation and learn from experienced developers.

3. Attend Events and Game Jams:

- o Game Jams: Short competitions to create a game in a limited time (e.g., Ludum Dare, Global Game Jam).
- o Conferences: Attend events like GDC (Game Developers Conference) or local meetups to network with professionals.

11.5 Pursuing Game Development as a Career

1. Job Opportunities:

   - o Look for roles like:
     - Game Developer
     - Game Designer
     - Technical Artist
     - QA Tester
   - o Build a strong resume that highlights your game development projects.

2. Freelancing:

   - o Offer your skills as a freelance developer or artist on platforms like Upwork or Fiverr.
   - o Create small games or tools for clients to build your portfolio and earn income.

3. Starting Your Own Studio:

   - o Consider forming a team to create and publish indie games.
   - o Explore funding options like Kickstarter, Patreon, or grants.

11.6 Exploring Advanced Projects

1. Build a Multiplayer Game:

- o Add networking features to your RPG using Python's socket library or frameworks like Photon.
- o Implement matchmaking, lobbies, and cooperative or competitive gameplay.

2. Create a 3D Game:

    - o Experiment with 3D engines like Unity or Unreal Engine.
    - o Learn 3D modeling tools like Blender to create your assets.

3. Develop a Game Engine:

    - o Build your own lightweight 2D engine as a personal challenge.
    - o Focus on rendering, physics, and input handling.

11.7 Continuous Learning

1. Stay Updated:

    - o Follow blogs, YouTube channels, or podcasts dedicated to game development.
    - o Example channels: Game Maker's Toolkit, The Cherno (C++ and Unity tutorials).

2. Take Online Courses:

    - o Platforms like Udemy, Coursera, or Codecademy offer courses on:
        - Game development
        - Python programming
        - Advanced algorithms

3. Experiment with New Technologies:

- o Explore AR/VR development using tools like Unity XR.
- o Experiment with AI integration for smarter NPCs or procedural content.

11.8 Expanding Your RPG

Revisit your completed RPG and consider implementing:

1. Online Multiplayer:

   Allow players to team up or compete with each other.

2. Modding Support:

   Enable players to modify or create new content for your game.

3. Mobile or Web Port:

   - o Adapt your game for mobile platforms using tools like Kivy or Unity.
   - o Convert it into a web game using libraries like Pyjs.

11.9 Conclusion

Game development is a journey of creativity, problem-solving, and continuous learning. With your RPG as a starting point, you've demonstrated the ability to design, code, and complete a project. By building on this foundation, learning new skills, and engaging with the community, you can grow into a skilled game developer ready to take on larger, more ambitious projects.

The journey doesn't end here—keep experimenting, creating, and sharing your work with the world. You've already accomplished so much, and the best is yet to come!

Chapter 12: Exploring New Horizons in Game Development

After completing your RPG and mastering the foundational skills of game development, it's time to look ahead. Chapter 12 focuses on advanced concepts, exploring emerging technologies, and setting yourself apart in the competitive field of game development. Whether you're planning to create more games, start a studio, or innovate with cutting-edge tools, this chapter will guide you in expanding your horizons.

12.1 Exploring Emerging Technologies

1. Artificial Intelligence (AI):

    o Implement advanced AI for NPCs and enemies:

        ▪ Use machine learning to create adaptive AI that learns player behavior.
        ▪ Example: Enemies that change tactics based on the player's combat style.
    o Experiment with natural language processing (NLP) for dynamic dialog systems.

2. Virtual Reality (VR) and Augmented Reality (AR):

    o Create immersive experiences using VR tools:

        ▪ Platforms: Oculus SDK, SteamVR, or Unity XR Toolkit.

- Example: An RPG where players interact with characters in a fully immersive 3D environment.

  o Explore AR for mobile RPGs:

    - Platforms: ARKit (iOS) or ARCore (Android).
    - Example: Use AR to place game characters in the real world.

3. Blockchain Gaming:

   o Explore the integration of blockchain for player-owned assets or decentralized marketplaces.
   o Example: Allow players to trade in-game items or currencies securely.

1. Procedural Generation:

   o Generate endless levels, quests, or worlds using procedural generation algorithms.

   o Tools and concepts:

     - Perlin noise for terrains.
     - Cellular automata for cave systems.
     - L-systems for generating realistic forests.

12.2 Diversifying Game Genres

Expand your portfolio by experimenting with different genres:

1. Platformers:

   o Create games with physics-based mechanics like jumping, grappling, or climbing.

- Example: A metroidvania with exploration and combat.

2. Puzzle Games:

    - Focus on designing logic-based challenges that test players' problem-solving skills.
    - Example: A time-manipulation puzzle game.

3. Roguelikes:

    - Implement procedural dungeon generation, permadeath, and character progression.
    - Example: A roguelike RPG with randomized enemies and loot.

4. Simulations:

    - Build management or simulation games with intricate systems.
    - Example: A farming simulator with dynamic weather and crop systems.

5. Multiplayer Games:

    - Explore online multiplayer mechanics:
        - Matchmaking, team play, and leaderboards.
        - Example: A co-op RPG where players team up to defeat bosses.

12.3 Improving Your Game Design Skills

1. Iterative Design:

    - Develop prototypes to test mechanics before committing to full development.

- Iterate based on feedback and playtesting.

2. Player Feedback:

    - Implement systems that respond to player actions dynamically.
    - Example: A morality system that alters the game world based on choices.

3. Storytelling Techniques:

    - Experiment with branching narratives or non-linear storytelling.
    - Tools: Twine for text-based games or Unity for complex dialogue trees.

4. Accessibility:

    - Design games that are inclusive for players with disabilities:
        - Subtitles for audio cues.
        - Customizable controls for mobility-impaired players.

12.4 Learning New Development Tools

1. Game Engines:

    - Expand your skillset to include other popular engines:
        - Unity: Ideal for 2D and 3D games with C# scripting.
        - Unreal Engine: Industry standard for high-end 3D games with Blueprints or C++.
        - Godot: Lightweight and beginner-friendly for indie projects.

2. Asset Creation Tools:

    o Create custom 2D and 3D assets:

        - Blender: 3D modeling, rigging, and animation.
        - Aseprite: Pixel art and sprite animation.
        - Substance Painter: Advanced texture creation.

3. Networking Frameworks:

    o Learn tools for creating online multiplayer experiences:

        - Photon Engine or Mirror for Unity.
        - Python's socket library for custom multiplayer systems.

12.5 Expanding into Cross-Platform Development

Reach wider audiences by releasing your games on multiple platforms:

1. Mobile Games:

    o Use engines like Unity or Godot to optimize for Android and iOS.
    o Example: A mobile RPG with touch-friendly controls.

2. Web Games:

    o Create browser-based games using libraries like:

        - Pyjs: Translates Python code into JavaScript.
        - Three.js: For 3D web games.

- Example: An RPG that runs directly in the browser.

3. Console Development:

    - Explore tools for porting your game to consoles:

        Unity or Unreal for Nintendo Switch, PlayStation, or Xbox.

    - Consider certification and publishing requirements for each console.

12.6 Building a Team or Studio

1. Collaborating with Others:

    - Form teams with artists, musicians, and designers to create larger projects.
    - Platforms for collaboration:
        - CrowdForge: Find collaborators for game development projects.
        - GameDev.net: Connect with other developers.

2. Starting a Game Studio:

    - Define your studio's mission and target audience.
    - Plan funding sources:
        - Crowdfunding platforms like Kickstarter.
        - Game grants or incubators.

3. Marketing and Branding:

- Create a recognizable brand for your games:

  Design a logo, website, and social media presence.

- Build a community:

  Engage with players through Discord or newsletters.

12.7 Pursuing Advanced Education

1. Formal Education:

   - Consider degrees or certifications in:
     - Game Design
     - Computer Science
     - Art and Animation

2. Online Courses:

   - Expand your knowledge through platforms like:
     - Udemy: Advanced game design or programming courses.
     - Coursera: University-level game development programs.

3. Game Development Books:

   - Read industry-standard books:
     - Game Programming Patterns by Robert Nystrom.
     - Level Up! The Guide to Great Video Game Design by Scott Rogers.

12.8 Participating in Game Jams

Game jams are a fun way to challenge yourself, collaborate with others, and explore new ideas.

1. Global Game Jam Events:

    o Examples: Ludum Dare, Global Game Jam, or GMTK Game Jam.
    o Time-limited challenges encourage creativity and rapid prototyping.

2. Benefits of Participation:

    o Meet other developers.
    o Learn to work under pressure.
    o Add unique projects to your portfolio.

12.9 Planning for the Future

1. Set Long-Term Goals:

    o Define your vision as a game developer:

    Example: "Launch a multiplayer RPG within 2 years."

2. Explore New Game Genres:

    Experiment with niche genres like rhythm games, survival horror, or educational games.

3. Stay Inspired:

Regularly play and analyze games to understand evolving trends.

12.10 Conclusion

Game development is a constantly evolving field with endless possibilities for innovation and creativity. By exploring emerging technologies, collaborating with others, and continuously refining your skills, you can push the boundaries of your capabilities. Whether you dream of creating groundbreaking indie games or joining a major studio, the skills and experience you've gained so far are a solid foundation for success.

The future of game development is yours to shape—keep experimenting, learning, and creating!

www.ingramcontent.com/pod-product-compliance
Lightning Source LLC
Chambersburg PA
CBHW071109240526
45469CB00006BD/2404